#45518

MW01045852

Walkingsticks

by Helen Frost

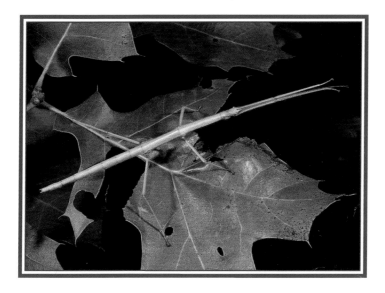

Consulting Editor: Gail Saunders-Smith, Ph.D.

Consultant: Gary A. Dunn, Director of Education,
Young Entomologists' Society

Pebble Books

an imprint of Capstone Press
Mankato, Minnesota

Pebble Books are published by Capstone Press
151 Good Counsel Drive, P.O. Box 669, Mankato, Minnesota 56002
http://www.capstone-press.com

2 3 4 5 6 06 05 04 03 02

Library of Congress Cataloging-in-Publication Data
Frost, Helen, 1949–
    Walkingsticks/by Helen Frost.
    p. cm.—(Insects)
    Includes bibliographical references (p. 23) and index.
    ISBN 0-7368-0854-X
    1. Stick insects—Juvenile literature. [1. Stick insects.] I. Title. II. Insects
(Mankato, Minn.)
QL509.5 .F76 2001
595.7'29—dc21   00-009800

Summary: Simple text and photographs describe the physical characteristics and
habits of walkingsticks.

Note to Parents and Teachers

The Insects series supports national science standards on units on
the diversity and unity of life. The series shows that animals have
features that help them live in different environments. This book
describes walkingsticks and illustrates their parts and habits. The
photographs support early readers in understanding the text. The
repetition of words and phrases helps early readers learn new
words. This book also introduces early readers to subject-specific
vocabulary words, which are defined in the Words to Know section.
Early readers may need assistance to read some words and to use
the Table of Contents, Words to Know, Read More, Internet Sites,
and Index/Word List sections of the book.

Table of Contents

Walkingsticks 5

Body 9

Head 13

Day and Night 17

Words to Know 22

Read More 23

Internet Sites 23

Index/Word List 24

Walkingsticks are insects that look like twigs.

walkingstick

Walkingsticks live on plants and in trees. They use camouflage to hide from predators.

8

Walkingsticks are
long and thin.

10

Walkingsticks are green or brown.

eyes

Walkingsticks have
a small head and
two small eyes.

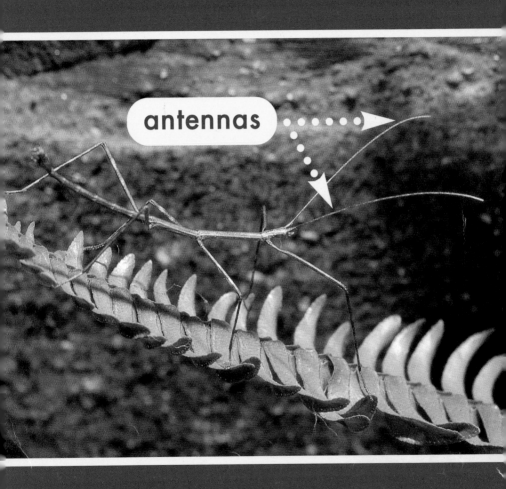

antennas

Walkingsticks have
two long antennas.

16

Most walkingsticks
stay still during the day.

Most walkingsticks move
and eat plants at night.

20

Some walkingsticks can shed a leg if a predator grabs it. Walkingsticks can escape from the predator and then grow a new leg.

Words to Know

camouflage—coloring that makes something look like its surroundings

escape—to break free; some walkingsticks can shed a leg to escape from a predator.

insect—a small animal with a hard outer shell, three body parts, six legs, and two antennas; walkingsticks are insects; about 2,000 kinds of walkingsticks live in the world.

predator—an animal that hunts and eats other animals; birds, lizards, and mice are predators of walkingsticks.

shed—to let something fall off or drop off; some walkingsticks can shed a leg if they are attacked; some walkingsticks can grow a new leg, but the new leg is not as strong as the first leg.

twig—a small, thin branch of a tree or other woody plant; walkingsticks blend into their surroundings because they look like twigs.

Read More

Green, Tamara. *Walking Sticks.* The New Creepy Crawly Collection. Milwaukee: Gareth Stevens, 1997.

Merrick, Patrick. *Walkingsticks.* Chanhassen, Minn.: Child's World, 1998.

Richardson, Adele. *Walking Sticks.* Bugs. Mankato, Minn.: Smart Apple Media, 1999.

Internet Sites

Bugbios: Walkingsticks
http://www.insects.org/entophiles/phasmida

Indian Walkingstick
http://www.EnchantedLearning.com/subjects/insects/orthoptera/Indianwalkingstick.shtml

Northern Walkingstick
http://www.pma.edmonton.ab.ca/natural/insects/projects/stickins.htm

Index/Word List

antennas, 15
brown, 11
camouflage, 7
day, 17
eat, 19
escape, 21
eyes, 13
grab, 21
green, 11
grow, 21
head, 13

hide, 7
insects, 5
leg, 21
live, 7
long, 9, 15
move, 19
night, 19
plants, 7, 19
predator,
  7, 21
shed, 21

small, 13
still, 17
thin, 9
trees, 7
twigs, 5
two, 13, 15

Word Count: 83
Early-Intervention Level: 12

Editorial Credits
Mari C. Schuh, editor; Timothy Halldin, cover designer; Kia Bielke, production
  designer; Kimberly Danger, photo researcher

Photo Credits
Barrett & MacKay, 14
James P. Rowan, 1, 10
Kay Johnson, 12
Leonard Rue Enterprises, 6
Lynn M. Stone/Bruce Coleman Inc., 16
Robert & Linda Mitchell, cover
Unicorn Stock Photos/Dede Gilman, 8
Visuals Unlimited/Doug Sokell, 4; Ken Lucas, 18; W. J. Weber, 20

24